Kaleidoscope Emotion

Shannon Kanaly

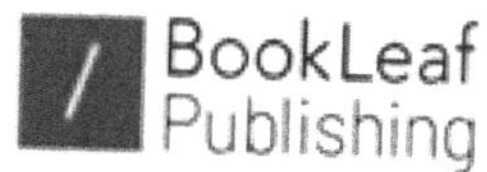

Presentation by *BookLeaf Publishing*

Web: www.bookleafpub.com

E-mail: info@bookleafpub.com

ISBN: 9789357213332

First edition 2023

DEDICATION

Lily- may you always find the courage to follow your dreams.
Eva- thank you for helping me follow my dreams and supporting me every step of the way.
Mom and Dad- thank you for encouraging me to explore everything in life and helping me find my love for writing.

Anxiety Attack

Sun shining through the panes,
A soft glow fills the room.
An internal storm brews.
Temperature rises;
Anxiety untamed.
Pressure increasing on the inside;
Weight of the warmth pressing down.
Rosy hot plate cheeks
Lungs unable to fill,
Gasping for thin weighted air.
Sweat dripping down
Melting like a crayon
Morphing into a soup puddle of hot wax.
Clenching fist,
Making crescent moon palm wounds;
Fighting for a breath.
Heart thumping
Thoughts running
Eyes close for a moment
Searching for a moment's break.
Fire dancing on skin,
Every nerve screaming
Standing to wobbly feet,
Tear filled eyes searching for a pane,
Instead locating a door.

Hand tightly grasping,
Twisting the knob.
Sweaty palms
Difficult to grasp.
Last ounce of energy,
Gentle push
Door open
Cool air on fire skin
Air crisp and clean
Sun shining,
Soft glows
Water evaporating
Heart thumps slow
Lungs able to fill
Anxiety tamed.

Maybe Like A Waterfall

Click of my pen
New sheet of paper
Motionless silence surrounds.
It's time again,
To let words flow;
Like a stream,
Maybe a waterfall.
Out of the mind
Down the arm
Through the pen
To the paper
Creating words
For others to feel;
To feel something.
Anger, joy, laughter,
Something one can relate.
Like a babbling brook,
Smooth transition over rocks,
My words will flow.

A paddle

I need you,
Like a canoe needs a paddle.
I love you,
Like bees love honey.
We go together,
Like peanut butter and chocolate.
Without you,
I am just a paddle smeared with peanut butter,
Being chased by bees.

Rear View Mirror

A drop in my stomach,
Just by your face.
Nervous energy
Restless body.
Unknowing what I did,
Unsure of what happened.
Once a friend
Now a memory.
Countless self questions
Answers received
Does it really matter?
You took to exit out of our friendship
Vanished into thin air.
When I saw you,
In that rear view mirror
I smiled.
That's where you belong.

Impossible List

Tangled in a web
Anchored to the floor
Unfinished list of tasks
Wraps like a bow.
Chores
Responsibilities
Work
Family
The list goes on.
The list is endless.
Boiling points met within,
Ticking bomb ready to explode.
Muscles tight
Holds the list.
Some tasks large,
Some small.
What if you don't succeed?
Impossible list.
It's ok,
Breathe in deep.
No matter the task,
The sky isn't on fire.

Departing Sun

Crisp autumn leaves
Crunch under my boot.
Damp chill
Wood burning
Sunlight departing
Darkness creeps in.
Dark closets
Locked doors
Whisper silent screams.
The time is coming
Sadness takes hold
A mark leaving grip
An inescapable torture.

Next Year

Tomorrow I'll finish that.
Tomorrow I'll do that.
Tomorrow I say!
Tomorrow tomorrow tomorrow.
When does tomorrow turn into yesterday?
Then yesterday turns into the day before?
When will tomorrow be today?
Next year I say!
When does the future become the present?
Or the present become a memory?
I don't know I say.
Is someone guaranteed tomorrow?
Or even today?
No one I say.
Tomorrow when will you do that?
Will it be today or next year?
Today I say!
Because tomorrow, next year
Is not a guarantee.

Things I've Lost

Lost time
Tick of the clock.
Found moments
Of unimaginable brilliance.
Lost friends
Silenced words between us.
Found self worth
Through cheek burning tears.
Lost weight
Pants barely hanging on.
Found confidence
Knowing one's worth.
Lost keys
Doors to not open.
Found path
A journey taken.
Lost myself
Time has passed.
Found myself
Time is now.

Voodoo Doll

Someone make me a doll.
The kind that when you rub it's back,
I get a glorious massage.
Crack it's back
Because mine isn't straight.
Whisper kind words
So I can hear them.
Tuck it in at night
Then maybe I can sleep soundly.
Someone get me a doll.
Take care of it.
Water it with love and good intentions.
Speak soft words
For flowers to bloom.
Someone get me a doll.
I can learn a thing or two.
To stop.
To take care of me
To speak kind words in the mirror
To watch myself blossom.
Until then,
Someone get me a doll.

Ocean

Sandy toes
Crashing waves
In rhythm;
Like a choreographed dance.
Moon directs
Sun shines brightly.
Shells come ashore;
A collectors dream.
The ocean,
Mighty and powerful
Unexpected and like clockwork.
Yet gentle and calming.
An unsolved mystery
On its mood.
Beautiful and wild.
Everyone sees her differently.

Kaleidoscope Emotion

Life is
Like a kaleidoscope.
Full of color,
Different shapes,
Twists and turns.
Onto a blank canvas,
Blast of color.
My life can be,
Washed in grey,
No expression
Heart dead,
Barely pumping.
Lack of energy.
Still alive
Corpse dragging
Each day
Longing for
That kaleidoscope view.

Mirror Glances

Glances in the mirror,
Aged 10 years.
Eyes wrinkled
No longer in college
Adult, not young adult.
Where is that line drawn?
Begins where?
Ends at what point?
Questions asked oneself.
Glances in the mirror,
Aged another 10 years.
Where has time gone?
Wisdom lines like delicate cloth
A middle aged adult.
When did that happen?
How to solve this aging one asks.
Stop glancing in the mirror.

Battery Operated

Ring the alarm
Like a robot
Lift from a slumber.
Another day
Knees crack, hips stiff.
Eyes crusted shut.
Back uneven,
Feet searching for a safe spot to step.
Same thing
Everyday.
Ready in 20
Out the door in 10
Robot is as robot does.
Same thing, knees crack.
Everyday.
Arrive home
Eyes closing quickly
Sweep with the uneven back
Wash with feet unsure
Ring the alarm.
Like a robot
Sink into a slumber
With heavy eyes
Hips stiff
For another day
In this robot life.

Love Grabbing Shirt Collar

The love that grabs you by the shirt collar
Pulls you in close
A romantic butterfly race in your digestive track.
Palms clammy
Heart doing jumping jacks
Feet ready for a marathon.
Hand nestled in mine
Arm around pulling me in close.
Clock stops.
It's just us.
Strangers faces turning into a sea
Blended emotions with mixed expression.
Remaining, just us.
Standing side by side and hand in hand,
Side glances to each other
Smile quickly forming
Turns to me
I grab his shirt collar
Pull him in close
Plant one on him,
in the endless expression of smiling faces.
Transformed like a movie
Except this is my real life.
A love that grabs you by the shirt collar.

Darling, A Word

Worried of others thoughts
Anxiety on the rise.
Trying to fit in,
To blend in.
Unsuccessful.
Failed attempt.
Would you like to try again?
Should I try again?
New goal.
Stop mixing in a mixing bowl.
Especially when you are an ingredient to stand
alone.
Stop morphing into a square,
When your suppose to be a triangle.
Stop worrying what others think,
When it's really none of your business.
Be yourself,
Shine bright,
Be greatness!
Darling, your meant for so much more.
Don't let them change you.
You were placed on earth for a reason
Go now
And just be.

Grief

Grief; the heartbreak of a lifetime.
Multiple stages
Drowning in salty tears
Denial of it all.
Anger flushed cheeks
Wishing they return.
Heartache that breaks you.
Pieces scatter the floor,
A hole in your chest
Gasping for air
Between breaths
Barters with a higher power
Doing anything for them to return.
Life is not that simple.
Lay them to rest
Looking down where they will be
Missing them terribly.
If your lucky
Someone lends a hand
Puts pieces back together with you.
Acceptance
Physically gone
Emotionally present
Each day within us.

Wiser Hopefully

There comes a moment
When everything shifts.
You are older now
Wiser hopefully
More lessons learned
Most certainly.
You look back
Glimpsing into the past
Longing for moments again.
Missing friends,
Family
Even missing once strangers.
Pro tip-
You can't go back
Only forward.
Trying to spark old friendships
Be prepared,
Nothing might change.
It's ok to be sad
Don't unpack there.
Keep going forward
New strangers will appear
Turns into a friend
All in due time.

Summer Day

Warm air
Shorts and t-shirts
Swats mosquitos
Wind caressing my face
Waves rolling
Sand between my toes
Campfire aroma
Adventure awaits
Vegetables grow
Leaves rustling from silent winds
All in a summers day.

Two Choices

There are times in our lives
Where we come to a screeching halt
Bumps in our path
Road block says
"You shall not pass"
Left with two choices.
Turn around or
Move forward.
Take your time deciding this.
Choices big or small
Design who we are.
Piece of advice
If you turn around,
That's ok.
Opportunities will rise
Just like the Sun each day.
If you move forward
I give you patience.
Seek alternative route
Rerouting to final destination
And don't forget,
Enjoy the journey.

Slay

Walk
Head held high
Strut like it's your job
Confidence dripping from your pores.
Radiating self love
From the core structure.
Internally shaking
Externally solid formation.
Slay the room
Mouth dropping
Surprised faces
Introduce the new you
Hello I say
Firm handshake
To my past self.
I'm here,
To teach you.
You will slay queen
Simply because you can.
You might be past me,
But thankfully I know
The next chapter.
Filled with confidence
Self love
Slay queen, slay.

Ups and Downs

My life has changed
For the better.
I have ups and downs
Attempting not to stay in the down.
To bathe in the ups
To live each day fully.
On the down,
I grab myself,
Wake up fool.
What are you doing?
Shakes out the doubtful mind,
The uncertainty of self.
Strength gathered
Starts the climb
A steep staircase
Filled with twists and turns
An inescapable maze.
On the way up to the sky
Filled with grace,
Full of life.
Lightweight like a feather.
What I remember;
In both places
I am successful.